Nene and CJ
The Big Blended Family

Ebony Hedgepeth
Illustrated by Terrence-X

WestBow Press books may be ordered through booksellers or by contacting:

WestBow Press
A Division of Thomas Nelson & Zondervan
1663 Liberty Drive
Bloomington, IN 47403
www.westbowpress.com
1 (866) 928-1240

Scripture taken from the New King James Version®. Copyright © 1982 by Thomas Nelson. Used by permission. All rights reserved.

ISBN: 978-1-9736-8018-5 (sc)
ISBN: 978-1-9736-8019-2 (e)

Library of Congress Control Number: 2019918693

Print information available on the last page.

WestBow Press rev. date: 11/20/2019

WESTBOW
PRESS®
A DIVISION OF THOMAS NELSON
& ZONDERVAN

Dear Reader,

This book is to help children understand that there are other children around the world who have blended family homes. It is okay for children to miss their siblings when they are away. It is okay to express those feelings to their parents.

"May the Lord watch between you and me when we are absent one from another. " – Genesis 31:49

Nene is Five and Cj is four.
Nene is short for Nehemya.
CJ is short for Cephas Jr.

They live with their Mommy and Daddy.

Nene and Cj have two older brothers
and three older sisters. There
are seven children in all.

As a family they do a lot of
fun things together.
They go to the park.

They go swimming at the pool and they make sand castles at the beach.

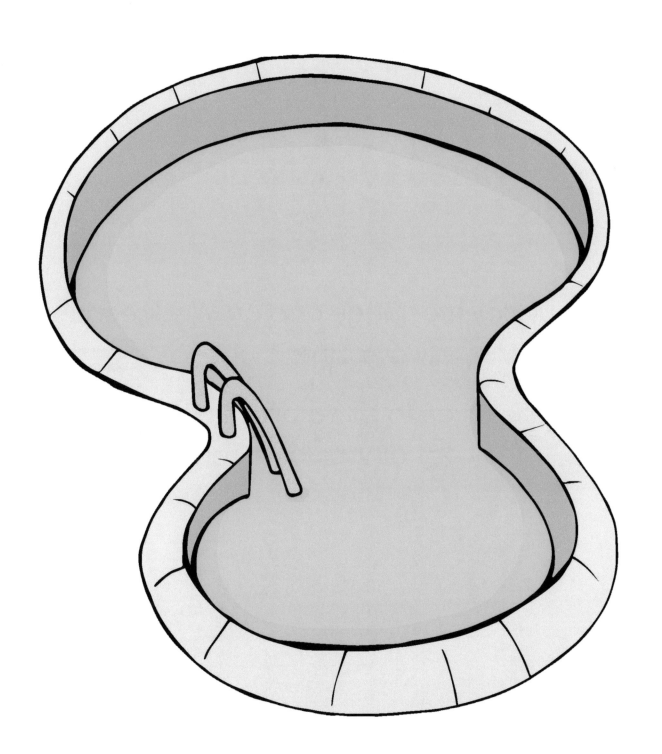

On Sunday mornings and on Wednesday evenings they always attend church together.

Nene loves to say a prayer before they eat dinner as a family.

But sometimes when Nene and Cj get home, the rest of their siblings' are not there.

The two of them run through the house calling their brothers' and sisters' names.

They even peek in all the rooms in the house but no one is there.

Nene and Cj are young and do not understand that they share the same dad but their mommy is a step mommy to the other children. The other children leave to spend time with their mothers.

They tell them their siblings will be back home soon. Even when their siblings are gone they are still a family.

A few days later all of their brothers
and sisters come back home and
Nene and Cj get filled with joy.

Author Biography

Ebony Hedgepeth currently lives in Newport News, Va. She is a military brat who moved around throughout her childhood to various countries. Her education includes a Master's Degree in ITM and BFA in Graphic Design. She works full-time and Also has her own business called Passionate Design and Paint. She is married to Cephas Hedgepeth. A loving mother to Nehemya and Cephas Jr., as well as a loving step mother to Nasir, Ahmir, A'Nyiah, Ja'Nyiah and Jaida. She is the daughter of Ron and Arlene. Ebony comes from a blended family and she is the younger sister of Latwanda, Monique and Ron Jr. She also is an aunt to many nephews and nieces. Ebony loves God and loves to help others. Her passion for her blended family gave her the desire to share her families experiences with the world. By having written this book, Ebony hopes families will read it together and it will be a great conversation starter about their own blended families. Be Blessed.

Printed in the United States
By Bookmasters